£2

HAUNTED BY HISTORY

To Jane Joseph, My Mother
Woman of Spirit,
Independence and Courage

Haunted
By
History

Poetry

By

Joan Anim-Addo

MANGO PUBLISHING
1998

© Joan Anim-Addo and Mango Publishing 1998

First published 1998

Published by Mango Publishing, London UK
P.O. Box 13378, London SE27 OZN

ISBN 1 902294 03 3

British Library Cataloguing in Publication Data
A CIP catalogue record for this book is available from the British Library

Printed in the UK by Watkiss Studios Ltd, Biggleswade

Cover design by Reggie Freeman, based on a painting by Fayel, 1970

CONTENTS

Past/ Somewhere Between/ Present

PRESENT

PAST

Talkee Mary's Lucid Moment

Whose blood red up the water so
whose blood
was it the women's menstrual flow
pulled all at once by the moon
falling like a shower
of crimson cacti flowers into the ocean

whose blood
was it the children's umbilical cord
fresh again   tugging at the womb's lining
preparing the life sac   expelling the poison
oozing so rich   redder than the redwood dyes

Tell me   whose blood
the warrior's perhaps   spilt on some field
where our magic   too weak   failed
and the gods exacting their claim
in ritual outpouring drop after steady drop

whose blood
Kwabena my son-o   Kofi my son-o   Kwesi my son-o
always behind these too heavy wrinkled eyelids
you hover   clear of the ship's side
arms like soft wings testing the air

My birds   your cries pierce the wind as at birth
and if you drop into the ocean's hungry maw
it is but part of the journey
Only   your cries   shred my heart

burn like pepper in the raw wounds of fresh hurt
but tell your sister   I'm coming back to Guinea
Wherever this ship disgorges me   I'm coming back
I'm coming

A Coastal Tribeswoman Recalls

It begins, a sunbleached cloth
billowing on dried bramble
but nearer and larger it looms.
Women gather their children
within dusty compound yards;
forbid their straying.
But the men, traders,
talk of every person's price
in grain, yams or cattle, finest gold dust
or the invader's life stealing rifle.

They who have outlawed fear
drink lustily in the evening's heat
trading in conquered peoples;
traditional enemies, criminals.
Man must live, they say,
by the sword, by the gun.
So whole villages emptied; delivered up
as those with pale eyes
return, speaking different tongues,
plying wares of indifferent quality.

Our men, too many big eyed;
too many heedless of consequence
spoken by those they call weak,
beat away the ghosts of their brothers;
wash away their sisters gnawing cries
with stronger spirits on the tongue.

It ends with the myriad tongues of this land
a dumb galaxy silenced over centuries.
You ask which came first: greed or violence?
Old enough to love unashamedly, I say:
To answer the riddle, let each seek out
the harsher lessons of our history.

Creation Story

In that beginning
there was silence
not the silver singing
silence that reassures
but a blue purple
wailing chasm
eerie with
the stuff of nightmares -
loss, dislocation,
enforced transportation,
bestial servitude -

Silence held, too,
simply because
people's tongues
had been cut off.

Time passed.
The rooted stump grew.
Misshapen it grew
learnt to curl anew
around curious consonants
to net strange vowel sounds;
to travel new routes.

Now in a space she claims
that feels sometimes
like home
a woman poet
of the new tongue
at evening time
sings alone.

And whilst others not too distant
hearing notes of fluid pain
pause puzzling
she gives voice
that soars on high calling
won't you, won't you
trace the scars of my knowledge
with your fingers
to begin our knowing?

Curse Of The Admiral

Curses? We have known them all.
At history's turn
the magic three, our way, fell.
The Pinto, *The Nina* and *The Santa Maria*.

Our people a blunt truth tell:
The ill wind
that blew them hither
brought more than our share of hell.

Europe's adventure - our loss -
taught protection in signing the cross
but only the magic "Zafa!"* is match
against that curse.

For fear of the fucu*, the Admiral's name
we will not sound. "Zafa!"
Earthquake, plane crash, explosions
are small, small expressions of the same.

Neither slavery nor genocide,
death by execution or a medal's pin-prick
could stem the tide of blight
through mean and meagre centuries.

Who celebrates this? Yet I heard a call
to celebration and "Zafa!" fell from so many lips
like parched corn popping
in so many glowing embers.

For the biggest curse of all,
the name that stays
is that of the Admiral
"Zafa!" the one we would erase.

*Zafa - word uttered as a charm/protection against a curse
*fucu- a terrible curse or blight

Mighty Benin

Beaten bronze depicts the spinning sun
bright witness to the texture of innocence
coming out of sixteenth century Africa.

Burnished swords on straight backed
warriors. Glorious Benin
and messengers bearing manillas.

See the locksman
on stout legs of a nation without fear.
He awaits the king's words.

Spinning flowers edge the shields
bad-oum, bad-oum, bad-oum
the heart of a proud nation.

Mighty Benin of panelled bronzes,
the owl sleeps on the shields
of the royal household.

Prepare the ceremonial horns
before the cries, the flashing swords
press closer the mark of the rope;

Before the traders redden the earth
and other ceremonies, other cries, other tongues
eclipse the spinning sun.

My Imoinda

Looking into her eyes
my soul takes fire;
soars to reach the sky.
Don't catch me;
let me rise until I fall again.
Don't catch me.

When I touch her skin,
so soft, tuned to such a sheen,
my fingertips glow.
I want to trace a trail
no snail will ever know
but just as slow a touch;
at least as slow.

Is that magic? If so tell me.
I haven't come across the like before.
Is that magic?
If so, then perhaps I ought to know.

Heart Drum

Heart drum. Heart drum. Hush.
Hush or explode. Can one body bear more?
Heart drum. Heart drum. Hush.
Sound mocks me. Silence is a new friend now.

Heart drum hush; lie still, hush up
unless, unless you are the talking drum's
silent messenger from a world known once,
now struck dumb, dumbstruck by cold misfortune.

Heart drum. Heart drum. Hush.
Hush or explode. Can one body bear more?
Heart drum, heart drum hush.
Sound mocks me. Silence is a new friend now.

Silence is a drumbeat, so faint
you cannot hear a single wing beat.
Strain all you might, you cannot hear .
Heart drum. Heart drum. Hush. Silence is my friend.

Island History

This giant funnel sprouting rust buds
from blood fed soil;
this strange iron plant
is import from that other age
when the native in his canoe choked on fear
watching a whole line of ships bear down.
Pot-bellied sails billowed life or death,
fluttered urgent profit; urgent loss.

This iron funnel once topped
a giant wooden skeleton,
industrial monument dwarfing huts
that penned unrecognised humans.
It knew the acrid smell,
the taste of green limes
delivered in stained sacking
a patchwork of blood and skin.

Palm prints were left
that told a dub version
of the crucifixion story;
of resurrection flights back to old Guinea.
This funnel here belched daily
into the thick air, a thicker smoke
from green limbs
torn from their roots, to order.

At hand, dawn women, earth women
shaped head rags into kata,
fashioning a pad to buffer the load.
No maidens these. See, they carry trees
cut for fuel on their heads.
This funnel ate offerings
of the dark cane women
the grace in their steps unseen;

Did not notice
the whipcracks longest pause
when coarse oaths died and laughter
floated, so many singing bubbles
in the dancing breeze.
It was the hurricane of fifty-five
that brought this funnel crashing
to its knees.

Our World

Liverpool! Bristol! Spanish Town! Lisbon!
Yes. We have graced many ports with nakedness
and marked how our shame began.

A gap-toothed girl, brazen smiled, caught, laid months
wooden coffined among many. Was never the same
for knowning the yoke, the trek, the fort and all besides.

The renk, putrid smell below deck lingers a festering song
to man's inhumanity. And the ships we have known.
Jesus of Lubeck! Amistad! Hannibal! Zong!

Against the lashing sea we heard a sharper crack; whips
to poison history though we jumped the broomstick;
danced to a tune of terror enough to steal souls, seal lips.

Still we survived. Knew canefields. Survived. Picked
a path through diesel fumes of refrigerated banana boat.
Seemed then like freedom's perfume. Want forever
licked.

First pa, then ma followed, learnt the wearing of a coat
to collect tickets, sweep platforms, clean toilets.
Took the persistent 'No blacks.' Lived less; saved more.

Since, my child, we have journeyed so
then this world bearing our footprints is plainly ours.

Birth Song (August 1834)

Such promise in a foetal limb's imprint
marking sharp against her palm.
Is this an elbow? A heel? Free birth hints.
Young black mother exhaling slowly; calm.

Marking sharp against her palm,
new life that will never know slavery's stings.
Young black mother exhaling slowly; calm.
She savours pain veiled in hope biting sharp as it sings.

New life that will never know slavery's stings
quickening within her womb; urges separation.
She savours pain, veiled in hope biting sharp as it sings.
And so, life confirmed in cry summons a libation.

Quickening womb urges separation
and birth wearied she sighs a baptismal song.
So, life confirmed in cry summons a libation.
A baby to wear red beans; taste freedom awaited so long.

And birth wearied she sighs a baptismal song;
calls on the waters of five rivers. She would not forget
a baby to wear red beans; taste freedom awaited so long;
a baby in ancestral presence to wear the beaded amulet.

Calls on the waters of five rivers. She would not forget.
Is this an elbow? A heel? Free birth hints;
A baby in ancestral presence to wear the beaded amulet.
Such promise in a foetal limb's imprint.

Paul Bogle Remembered (1865)

Hot Sunday it was   bright like fire
Couldn't get a breeze anywhere
Not even to stir paper
Look how the words of the white Queen
Stay so flat   nailed against breadfruit trees
Whole day heat calling   calling

Hot Sunday it was
Everybody waiting for sun to drop
Out of she red dress   out of the sky
We looking a sign from the heavens
Telling why we must labour more
When slavery days done already

Hot Sunday   night fall black as coal
And way yonder shooting up from Bailey field
A sign to read the marks on paper
The advice from the wise Queen   meantime
Fire shooting sparks and answering fires
As far as the old eyes can see

Hot Sunday   Masanto on the Queen's advice
Island burning   If is land we want
We have to take   cause nobody giving
And the Lord is our shepherd   Gunshot or no
We shall not want   though they plan
New crosses for these old backs

Hot Sunday   sun gone to bed but heat rising
People running under cover of thorns
Crisscrossing cane fields   Jumping gullies
Against guns   catching brief words of comfort
We meet at Calvary in Morant Bay
This Sunday like Easter   Brothers   sisters today
It is our will   to construct our own crosses

Unsung Artists

Some place in pale blue space overhead,
the evening sky accepts always
the bowing and curtseying
of branches just so richly green

Connecting with universal time
ages past and those to come.
Yesterday, high clouds racing overhead
spoke of remembered-forgotten other time,

Of unsung women, this side of the Atlantic, who,
from insignificant strips of cane,
formed lacy edged mats - never quite finished -
certainly more elaborate than functional;

Women, who saw in dusky moths' wings
patterns which their hands released from labour
etched in the dirt patch that was 'de yard' -
no signature; no agents; no thought of market place -

Women who heard a song's chorus in the gurgling
of water over stone and hummed it back to the stars,
though survival, not composition, remained foremost;
remained ceaselessly sapping at creativity;

Women who reproduced eddying shadows
in the parting of hair for plaits slender as lizard's tails;
sorted dried beans, trawling certain reds
and marbled greens to adorn, later,

A baby's plumpish arm or, plunge
over unsupported breasts simply because
despite all, these were colours that fired the soul's
unrelenting search for expression

And women who, rocking a cradled head at day's decline
found their words pouring forth, like bats at twilight,
to shape a story that would surprise or please, regardless;
words of falling sustenance from full lips of unsung artists.

Incense Burner

Made of rich brass, time tarnished now
I carried, then, incense
thrown in long swings
the length of a man's arm
reaching past the King of Kings
to a God we have always known.

The tinkle of fifteen bells
fifteen fold today
would not summon our God.
Heedless of the covenant,
he has turned his back
on faithful Ethiopia.

Crossed. Our crosses crossed
we bear in silence
in brass filigreed silence
time blackened now
though our ebony priests first
lit a bold beacon light
to a world steeped in darkness.

Alas, the lion of Judah sleeps;
the children of Solomon disperse.
We struggle to keep war at bay
unable to dispel the flies
from ashen lips of those we love;
death from filmy eyes.

Swing the brass censer
with multiple bells
higher still.
Let voices fill
the empty domes
which God shuns.

Rude Fruit

Take Shakespeare's 'bastard Edmund', tragic son,
powerful sign through which we might understand
malice, vengeful stirrings, despotic thrust.
What of the bastard daughter? Here she stands.
No subterfuge. She says out loud, 'I am

The bastard daughter of the slave woman,
a memory of memories of needing
long occluded by the wilful rape
and her merely property after all.

I do not know my father, deny him
even as I have been denied.
His genetic corruption is poison
that will pervade no further
though a nugget of hatred remains.

I trumpet loss, pain, stunted growth
even as his proper part remains
unacknowledged through time, by him, her, me.
I am to be found thus cold steel tempered.

For what does a mother giving birth
to the rude fruit of rape perceive
as she looks matter of factly
through a shifting prism of unbidden tears
at life hitherto unwanted?

I, daughter of such union, such history,
how will I teach my offspring love?
What human miracle allows it all
to be put right, that I may pass on

Self respect and proper pride
to prepare an equal being for thriving in this world
and how many centuries will it take?
I cannot, will not wait. My child is due'.

New World Prize

The best man won? Come view the prize!
See. Mystery whispers in its dusky hue;
All the parts a woman need are there in view.
Take her as wish needs, under roofed space or open skies.

Note those buttocks; mark the size.
Mounds! She knows labour properly as beasts do.
The best man won? Come. View the prize!
See mystery whispering in its dusky hue.

Yet we are men of scruples. We tell no lies.
So if your conscience wrinkles a clearer hue
then, let your mistress have her and still so might you.
This one need never look you in the eyes.
The best man won. So, come view. The prize!
Mystery waits whispering in its dusky hue.

Ghost Of History

Yesterday, I saw her.
So, she too has traced this path?
I should have guessed the secret
shaped in the woodsmoke's guilty curl.
Here she cast sidelong glances at a dull pond
guessing after so many strange words
flung in the chasm between her and her world,
this was not the place to draw water.

Here, she slid through five barred gate,
caught at a drooping hem and steupsed so long
it puzzled a solitary pheasant.
There she wondered at the neat fence
trying, on this side, to contain the stream
and here she lingered in some stealth, curious
that pale moss balls grew in clumps
on a squat dark limbed tree that was not lime.

The bucket's handle closed on sapodilla skin
fingers used to so much labour
though new to so much chill, so much cold.
The dark well beckoned.
Here she drew water, studying new birdcall.
Three places, one home, same life but the call different
and so she lifted the stiff bucket to her head
shifted mud stained calico

clear of flagstones like grey bones and
bearing dignity with her load
sailed towards madame's new English home
against faint sniggers at an open casement.

Another African Tomb: Ilfracombe
(October, 1796)

Ku-kuum! Olokun! Yemoja! How many leagues to
Ilfracombe
where vengeful winds whip the guilty Atlantic waters?
Hear! The hull of a ship called *London* bears the beat of
stormy rhythms
in time to black gods' rage. Hear it still echoing ages
deep.
Ku-kuum! Break the iron fetters. Make room for a mass
grave! Make room!

How many? Olokun! How many leagues to Ilfracombe?
Here while Shango bellowed, Yemoja birthed a fiercer
seascape
of old Guinea. See the coastal fringes textured a frothing
red.
Ku-kuum! Olokun! Yemoja! Waves foam and crest; crash,
wash, break.
Take the bodies; black and white dancing equal in the
gloom.

Ku-kuum! How many leagues to Ilfracombe?
How many leagues, Olokun, from hell to damnation?
You answered, 'Damn you! Claim your bleached, beached
up souls for burial.
Guinea's children will trace this trail of bones back to your
very shores'.
Meantime, a trove of perfect teeth; of African skulls mark

Aunt Hetty - Other Mother
(after Mary Prince)

When first I came to this place
of heartless timber and cold stone
was black aunt Hetty's face
fuelled my childish needing.

She it was gave the odd kind word
the approving look rare enough
beside the cutting gaze of my mistress.
How Aunt Hetty oiled the mark of the cowskin whip.

She saw that my plate held meat.
She battled with tight knots lurking in my hair.
She reminded me a smile cost nothing
and how mamma would be 'rightly proud' of me.

They say, that despite all, when the night
fell like long black shrouds
off pale jalousied partitions
that ole devil whip claimed Aunt Hetty.

So now, the women rock; they moan low.
They talk of burying her within the sound
of the cane mill bell. I wonder where mama is
now Aunt Hetty's dry laugh fled this house. Gone.

Was That Sethe Or Her Sister?
(after Toni Morrison's *Beloved*)

Maternity figure of woman
on Ashanti stool
suckling child
- wooden, still -
milk-breathed
and at one.

Maternity figure of woman
other situation we know full well
no child to suckle. Child done gone.
Sold. Mother wooden - still -
too drained, too whiplashed.
A stone; no stool.

A stone is not a stool.
In this hard place
no comfort; no rest
where body thieves
separate sister, husband, infant
Even the wisdom of elders absent.

How to cook without a stool?
How to grind peppers for the pot
with earth spirit not knowing libation
and palm oil an acrid memory?
In this corner, the heart of man
is only stone

echo-ing a faint, faint
bu-dum, bu-dum, bu-dum.
So, infant body wooden now
stiff still. No to mothering
in this stone place.
No. No. No-oooh!
Howling into stone
On stone/ through stone
Maternity figure of woman
Wooden. Still.

Ade And Abena

Adam was an African they tell us.
The West changed his name. So, to
re-interpret slavery's degradation:
Kojo - or Ade - was really Adam.
But all of this was in a time pre-Freud and
no-one paid particular attention
to the kind of Oedipal behaviour
from Africa to the Americas
or the everyday raping of mothers.

Post cathartic; with technology's aid
we can afford, to discover, though late,
Mama Abena and Papa Ade
who lived in a place across wide waters
a space not unlike the old 'White Man's Grave.'
Though no-one recognised it at the time
this was the Garden of Eden itself.

Saraka

Drums sound! Saraka tonight!
Children come; old ones come.
Drums sound! Saraka tonight.
Come one; come all!

Tonight the children eat first
and the old people,
while candles shine within
and moon face bright, a challenge to evil.
To those who could not be here
a parcel of food wrapped in green leaves.
Tonight we feed the way -
conjoin with our ancestors who knew -
our hands tearing the food, dripping
rolling and sharing; at one.

Drums sound! Saraka tonight!
Drums sound!
Pass the boli; drink.
The beaten earth has tasted.
The cloth is on our head.
The wrap is around us holding us
holding us to the rhythm
we dare not forget.
We remember, yes, we remember.
Oh, the shameful thing has happened.
How could we forget?

Drums sound! Saraka tonight!
Drums sound!
The seas have churned over our brothers
our sisters who would, who would be free.
Blood has been spilt
again and again on this soil.
Mother! Guine-a! Oh, Guine-a weep forever
for your children stolen away.
Weep, oh ancestors, plene mwen,
Flood the parched earth.
We dance that the rhythms may be carried
above the sound of sorrow.

Drums sound! Saraka tonight!
Drums sound!
Oh mother, look, we are dancing.
Watch our bare feet shuffle
in touch with the earth.
See the rhythms you have taught us
and know that we will remember.
In this far off island place
witnessing what we could not speak
know your children have kept faith
our stories baked in the sun secrets like drumskins;
Your daughters now make drums.

Drums sound! Saraka tonight!
Drums sound!
Young mothers take a fresh bread roll
from the offering
to be wrapped in a clean cloth
and put away in your homes.

Let the children find them
stale and hard and ask why.
For when we forget, blood flows;
not the blood of old chickens
but of our children, ourselves.

Drums sound! Saraka tonight!
Drums sound!
Big drum!
Bula side drum!
Goatskin hands on drum!

Middle cot drum!
Drum sound!
Hele mwen plene!
Drums sound! Drums sound!

Somewhere Between

Last Toast On The *Empire Windrush*

'I cannot speak for how others choose.
Some say Canada; plenty opt for USA.
A loyal son of Empire, I prefer England.
This is my last toast so raise your glasses!'
Tots of rum; a galaxy of liquid moons
high in a darkening cabin with echoes of war.

For the Motherland called before. They came-
closed their ears to women's wailing -
Marched, whistled, up the gangway.
Brave boys they were in '44, uniform proud
adventure hungry. So much they could not know.

Never guessed death could come
in frost bitten toes or brawling off a bridge
whilst still in training. Never guessed how much
rice an' peas and calypso rhythms could be missed.
Still, some survived the action,
showed Hitler a thing or two. Survived.

And England calls again. This time to build. So,
they are proud to answer. Yes. Closed the little shop,
spent the savings on a passage to a
better tomorrow. Who knows?
The future is theirs to pick, choose and refuse.
They can be anything. The Motherland beckons.

Ship's motion ceases; a bottle raised.
'My tie is straight, my hat just so', says Winston
'and see your face in the shine of my shoe.
One last toast! To the Motherland! The Future!
I know about the cold; the winters to come.
There can be no surprises for me. Not this time'.

Separation

banana boat blocking out de sun
filling de harbour
slick sea heaving dark
under rotting jetty boards
more people gathered
dan in de market place
something happenin

up the gangway
carrying grips and bulky parcels
big people voices filling de air
and a pressin and a jammin
smart shoes   sharp pressed pants
and hats here more than church
I can't quite understan

inside we snake corridors
suitcases bounce   doors fling open
we movin with the tidal drag
somebody call out   we turn and follow
inside de small place   it quiet
no sun   no people   no air
just me an me little sister

de small cry turn to big bawling
to terror exploding, busting
the dense universe apart
with me at the small   small space
in the dark centre   I am the iris
in my little sister's frightened eyes
we goin away from we home

uncle's voice hardens
demands sensible behaviour
he have to go look bout de cattle
I say   de place dark dark
voices mix with laughter
a light switch on   see he say   but
I grip uncle's hand tight   tighter   tighter

If I Should Call Her Muse

The tongue I would hear
she did not speak. So,
I denied her presence
saying
'Old lady don't follow me
this is my busy time
my youth.'
But she waited
folding her black angel's wings
so tight I did not see.
She waited.
I think she must have stayed
hugging evenings' shadows
like some hopeful lover
waiting, watching. In truth
I never noticed.

Waking one day from the long sleep
I found her
like one finds a fragrance
on a flower that has always stood there.
Patience shone from her eyes,
no sorrow. No rebuke. She spoke softly.
This time I heard. I knew her.
She is with me still.
She is with me.
And if I should call her Muse
would you
know her?

Drummer From Back Home

The drummer from back home
beats a hurricane rhythm.
Tough hide palms cracked,
he labours stick on skin of talking drum
squeezes her waist
tender but urgent.
Now, now the orgasmic thrust.

The drummer from back home
rhythms a golden Ashanti stool
before their eyes. Their glorious past
lives. No ex-colony this.
Women ululate; men sip strong liquor
forgetting affairs of state.

The drummer from back home
returns to his shack, the Koran
seven girl children but no boys.
Two wives wait with empty rice jars.
What use music to hungry bellies?
He empties his pockets of crumpled notes
scrapes together the useless coins
to a tongue lashing for selling his skills short.

The drummer from back home
turns to the solace of the bar, fresh palm wine
drunk to the rhythm in his head.
He confides again to anyone who listens
he'll be going to the West soon, London or New York
don't mind where. He awaits the letter from cousins.
There, in the West, he says, artists are always
paid their worth, in good gold. Always.

Thoughts From A Cricket Orphan

I wonder which girlchild could forgive
a mother's leaving her for cricket.
She should have known how such absence stretches
like the long, fearful hand of the jumbie
into fretful childhood dreams. I waited.

Doubtless she stood at the crease eyes alert
to the streak of red, air-borne or on pitch,
seeking the boundary. I watched sunset reds
like layered hair ribbons touched by night's stain
waiting her return. Such

Devotion to hard leather on willow
is strange behaviour in a mother.
And when she was at home, dissatisfied
I listened to her voice made for stories
debating unendingly unto sleep
the intricacies of the LBW.

I picture her now, in cream flannels
made in skirted days for mums
at the old Singer, the treadled one
'so much more reliable
than these electric things.' Gran's words.

I see her, plaits awry, gran's constant cry
'She must always behave like a boy !'
Her girl. No time for dolls or housey house-y games
- such shame - but give her a coconut bat
and anything would do for a ball.

Yet that cold imperative 'chores first' held
then as now. Did she practise in secret
those skills denied to girls
skills she craved? Mine remains
a grudging sympathy. I'll leave it be.

Then and to this very day
who get run out and who get duck
I never could care.
Under arm or over, fastbowl or spin
don't bother me. I always thought
this career for a mother
far from maidenly.

There Is Something About Rain

There is something about rain
whether washing red tiled roofs sparkly new
or making dark mirrors of grimy city streets
or spattering window panes
that look on blackened leafless trees in winter
or drumming on galvanised rooftops
crowning huts or boastful bungalows
or bouncing steadily on waiting leaves.

There is something about rain
that moves in slanted sheets
down hillsides round as a cat's curled back
rain slowly moving, solid, into the valley
while you watch from kitchen back steps
peering over the stable style door
wondering whether, when the sun comes out
there will be a rainbow
stretching over Uncle Eddie's house
or maybe even two rainbows
if it's a really lucky day.

There is something about rain
and I think that here, in these tamed forest islands
when the ancestors stood shackled
or bent in toil, again,
or tasted dust, again, the other end
of the whip's lustful sting

or witnessed blood trickling into the greedy soil;
when it rained in sheets like this
or fell suddenly out of an unobserved sky
sprinkling work burdened backs
mingling with their rough sweat,
these wronged, noble Guinea people
straightened enslaved bodies
connected with the earth
looked into the world's eye
feeling their green humanity
heedless of the dehumanising lies
the ever present abuse.

It is such knowledge
and this steady, insistent rain whispering
that, in foreign city or homeplace, keeps me,
offspring of those selfsame ancestors,
connected, at home, any place.

First Winter

Our first winter together, my child and I.
He moans in his sleep, feverish.
I chase away memories
of family left behind;
women who would know remedies
to bring a night fever down.
I turn up the paraffin heater
study its murky window; ignore its smell.

Our first winter together. My child coughs
hard in a tight chest; wheezes.
My chest heaves. I need a healing draught,
a breeze fresh off the sea
to stir and ease the heaviness
that weighs about us both.

First January smog. My child cries out.
Was it all for such greyness; such wintry life?
My soul cries out. I know at last
there is no great Listener
whom it may please to grant my wish.
My boy is still. I doze and wake to stillness.
I wait to see the battle out.

Our first winter together, my child and I.
I want to pray: teach me how to be
a good mother so that I have
the child who would not be sick
who would not each time die a little,
not in London; not in a heartless grey winter.

Belated Bouquet

We parted on a promise
that was not kept
and so she haunts me.

Still, it's the gentlest haunting
that I shall ever know
But that promise sworn

On childhood heart was sacred;
not forgotten. It is only that
despite my will, guilt-trapped,

Anger trapped, I remained
in this frozen place of need
for we were caught; poverty trap caught.

Now nagging maturity demands
I lay her soul to rest.
Grandmother, as well as tears

Accept this bouquet of words
from a favoured grand daughter.
Now rest; and so shall I.

Returning To The Family Church
(Grenada)

Bells clang. I climb wide stairs to church; do not
follow the thorn crushed path my mother takes.
That narrow trap along cobbled walkway,
still sharp edged, tripped my childhood stepping
to reach the meaner back doorway. I enter
through pillared porticoes, deep shadows, doubt.

Evensong waits. Bowed, older women
whisper urgent entreaties to God.
Those high caste, matching colouring,
no longer sit up front, stiff starched.
Crimplene and Terylene now hold sway
for church smart foreign outfits.

In the strained twilight I stroke cool wood,
a high backed pew, time polished black.
Not ebony, I guess. Likely,
English oak to grace these dimensions -
such fine exemplar of colonial
ecclesiastical architecture -

Searching the images in stained glass,
the statues, too, for meanings, I wonder
did just such dark wood ever grace
the holds of Liverpool or Bristol ships
triangle-bound? With what effect? In my
family church, I search in vain, for me.

You see, I am not at the altar end;
not in the thin voices straining
nor even in the incense drift
that bells, not drums pronounce.

Here pale witnesses stand candlelit guard
at each pale priest's solemn rehearsal.
Alabaster angels flanked by cut flowers
and saints with yellow cornsilk hair
watched here for centuries, how humbled subjects
paid homage to unknown kings and queens.
Something I know now, learnt through harsh lessons
of unbelonging, separates me at last from all this.

A Space Where Daggers Dance

Each night he threw down
the bundle of sticks
selected the choicest switch
one that would whistle
through the air
if he chose.

Sometimes he peeled the bark
stripped it blond
stripped it bare.
Time was his
for the taking
and later
he would make the air sing
with the whistling
of his whip
mixed with a wife's cries.

Still later he pulled her to him
his face set up
the whip still whistling
in his eyes
and she was his.
She would do his bedding;
he was Man.

Daughter grew to the vow
made on the back steps

between best girl friends
foreheads touching
in whispered earnestness.
"This life," they said
"of women beaten daily
must stop".

Daughter grew
carrying her mother's cries
in the warm space of her heart
so that her husband
approaching
with a flying fist one day
stopped in the path
of a steel blade
wedged in her hands
and daggers
dancing like devils
in her eyes.

Grandmother

My grandmother was a mermaid
retired from the sea
her hair still dripping sea secrets
and she sang.

She spun enchanted yarns
plucked from silver strands
of moonbeam flecked
to match the glints of water
mirrored in her hair.

She kept sea mementos secret
on bedroom shelves.
My small hands traced magic spirals
touched shells on pearled combs
and other mermaid's things

And when she sang
with the full moon calling
outside her window,
she covered her sea form
in flowing gowns
at night's excuse.

Hair let down from pinned plaits,
she brush stroked her waves
massaging the song

that would reach
those sisters left behind
- shimmering, sharp, shaft of a song -

My own flesh goose bumped.
I stroked the silken skin
of arms that fins replaced
and marked where scales like lace
had worn. I claimed her
My mermaid queen.

Popo Baby

Dont fret so Girlie dont you want look pretty
I goin plait some cornrow
Tailcomb long that meet in the middle
In a big tall pile just so
And when yu have red ribbon
Satin shining in a big bow
What yu think every body goin say
Dry yu eyes dem send de tears away

Dont fret so Girlie an yu mammie send yu
Pretty dandan wid jacket to match
And long sleeve like a big big ooman
And royal blue coat wid velvet collar
Mek yu hand tremble fuh touch it
Wot a smart young lady youll be tomorrow
When yu look in de glass an yu cut yu eye
Youll be like in picture book land no lie

So dont fret no more Girlie wot yu cryin for
An yu goin on big big ship wid Tantie Vie
Dey say dining an dancing wid silver fork
From morning till night dat is all yu doing for days
An the big engine just driving yu on regardless
To yu mammie yu still miss her an yu new daddie
If yu take on so Girlie wha lef for yu gran to do
Who yu tink should fret more popo baby me or you

Sisters

Two sisters sit on stone steps
one figure; a single picture in the falling light
mahogany brown with faded reds and yellows.
Four thick plaits
hang stiffly from drooping heads
twinned souls
bean curled a harmony of despondence.
Their eyes speak
only resignation
to situations
other than they were
mother
gone to find hard cash
brother
gone to find adventure
father
just plain gone.

They do not just now care to remember
colours on fabric
breathtaking beneath layers of tissue
finer than new corn silk
layers of guilt
postmarked overseas.
Gone now the dimpled gap toothed smiles
the energy translated to dance

accompanying joyous music of colours
in a new frock held in front of the mirror
a first time.

Two sisters sit on stone steps
resigned to finding each other
through time that stretches
taut like the brown skin
on their young faces
finding each other
or losing themselves.

A Whole Pin

George take a shiny new pin
walk over to his wife new housecoat
lace still stiff round the edge
pockets standing out like they full
guava flesh buttons
in a neat long row and
pinching the seersucker gently
he fastened the safety pin,
turned to his new bride and said,
'when things go bad
yu all women always say
de man don't even give me pinhead.
Yu can never say dat to me, never.
Is not pinhead dis. No.
I give you a whole big pin
and it brand new'.

Storyteller

Like an ancient rug maker
nimble fingers
threading visions,
she weaves a tale so fine
so sad
so beautiful in the telling
of a people
with a history so terrible
it could only be known
through story;
so painful,
only a song could capture it
without bruising those who heard.
And that people
with that history
you and I know
but the story so haunts still
that most of us
dare not speak it
even today.

Immigrant Woman

Caged now
weary eyes downcast
she pads familiar territory.
A gaze roadwards, mere habit,
confirms again these streets
not paved with gold, but litter.
Watching discarded packets
skitter along cracked paving,
she dreams;
the bait of hard currency recedes.
She dreams green fields and hills,
voices echoing laughter,
a hushed church,
textured lace on heads; Sunday hats bobbing.
She hears heels clicking closer to grace
and pulls to
adjusts her coat, an unfashionable blue,
forgets the fashioning
of that other life, a trap no less,
of mops, buckets, sometimes ladles,
where none see her
recognising only her function.
And there, under iron grey skies,
head tied against the cold and drab,
she murmurs prayers
and walks a moment, upright,
in quiet dignity
a fully valued being.

Scattered

I dreamt
I saw my family taken captive
snatched; packed tight
bundled like sticks for firewood
stored in dark places
airtight but for the stench of suffering
transported at length
to distant storm weary shores.

I dreamt
I saw my grandmother weep pearl tears.
Sold, raped, her silence
cried aloud for justice
in face of the moon's
full witness.

I dreamt
I saw my mother kept in bondage
iron sound of shackles
deafening her ears
to the cries of babes at her breast
my father reared stud in a stable
turned zombie by the whip.

I dreamt
I saw my sisters like ghosts in rags
search the highest brittle branches

of dying trees
for tongues
that they might call
my brothers home.

I dreamt?
But my family is scattered like leaves
blown in a hurricane
and my grandmother's final drumbeat
pulses the sombre reality
calling again
that it did
happen
that it did
which is why
we still
search for lost tongues.

Boat Train

Here in these padded pews
we receive processed packages of food
soft cheese in silver wrapped triangles;
crisps paper bag sealed
with a blue twist gift of salt thrown in.
We rock to the boat train's rhythm.

The English countryside: green and pleasant.
Yonder, thick smoke curling out of tall spouts.
We speak; receive blank looks. Mother-land! Mother-land!
My Sunday hat warms chilly knees.
Rocking to the boat train's rhythm
memory plays tricks. I think of you.

Choice

This dirt track at my back
travelled with unsteady feet
in greener days meets at narrowed points
thick with overhung branches, to whisper
secrets sprinkled with mottled light.

No amount of listening
has yet revealed
the timeless wisdom of these trees
nor in their shimmying do they let fall
half what I would wish to know.

You stand here, similar stance
before the fireflies' searching dance
before the cicadas' song
as you did when you belaboured
with just such a stick
this feather leafed gloriseta.
Which way? Though travelled, you cannot
close out the familiar landscape.

Last night you watched a flock of blackbirds
having mistaken their urgent calls
for seagulls' cries and followed blinkered eyes
searching their distant path. They left no sign.
Only unease remained; a certain lack
in human patterning.

Ahead, and on either side
tarmacced road beckons in the gloom,
dusky measure of our ripening
You stand now in silent plea
taut with the elastic pull
to turn again. You cannot close out
the familiar landscape.
Which way? With what consequence?
You stand poised, choosing.

Summer Mango

His hands hold steady past the spasm
and softly he bites this season's treat
a mango, its outer skin sunset streaked.
His lips have crafted petals. Pure Ashanti gold,
they hang where teeth had torn
revealing succulent flesh
full, buttery moon ripe.

He does not catch my eye
not wanting to think of here, of now.
The avenue of trees speak magic in the breeze
transporting him homewards-
sitting in the shade as his father always did
protecting his head from the sun-

He never wonders why he hears the sea gasp
and a young girl laugh calling him, 'Greedy!'
Her back towards him, he cannot make out her face.
But he can wait. The sun dips
Darkness will draw them closer.

Smiling, he watches her whilst the sun goes down.
And the breeze off the sea sculpting her slender legs
and worn cotton frock blows salt into his nostrils
obliterating that instant
the mango's consummate perfume.

Black hands, work all your life hands
unsteady now, savour memories
in a mango whilst time grows young again
on a park bench in Greenwich, in June.

PRESENT

A Room Of My Own

In this proud corner, six shelves
I measured for, bought, cut up, put up.
They bear chronicles of one black woman's history.
Where wall and wood do not quite meet
thin books fall off. They tumble, clattering
a five stringed guitar leaning against
so many pictures waiting to be framed.

The mantel piece, bric a brac crammed,
remains cloaked in dust
lending a furry coating
to the shoulders of blue vases
and translucent bottles
collected when time ranged uncluttered.

A square wall clock
fire engine red no longer keeps time
though the hands still move
to a rhythm of their own.
One matching wooden candlestick
stands alone, centre stage by default.

A slender ceramic jug glazed white
with terracotta peeping through
sprouts dried grasses some curled into apostrophes
with the burden of dust.
A curdled orange candle, volcano mouthed,
squats close, scented a fragrance of the sixties.

And topping the stack of sweet-tins, the plastic containers
securing used-only-once jars of make-up,
tiny shells from long ago places,
keys, screws, odd reels of thread
small raffia baskets and Stanley knife blades
a gold edged jar sits - once an ill fitting present-

It looks down now upon a bed of dark wood
carved end panels, fluted
and tapered into four acorn cups
and a frame declaring itself
'Wire mattress and bedstead makers
to his Majesty the King!'
My nearly royal relic wears flaming green
a duvet cover bisected by white tram lines.

Across the carnival red blue green carpet
dancing with green black peach curtains
A three foot Kelegele mask
lies abandoned in a corner
its etched zebra face crying 'Life! Life!'
The nearby metal trunk keeps its secrets.

It holds fabrics from Limbada's in Zambia,
from street bazaars in Mombasa,
bargains from Brixton market and early Habitat's,
plus treasured pieces from Grenada,
from my mother's old dressing gown
(just possibly my grandmother's.)
Chitenges lie beneath green squares

This room, first I ever had
and chose as my own, resists order, holds time
higgledy piggledy in old files, bags, baskets
from pre-adult years, before mothering, nurturing!
The mixed flowers honey from Mexico was a gift.

One day, maybe, I shall relish honeycomb.
Till then the Ashanti fertility doll remains hidden.
'Forget the womb,' I mutter. ' Only grant me a fertile mind.
At last I have a room of my own and I am learning
how to steal time.'

She Chants

The griot chants
memories dance
tropical rain flows
ravine swells
dizzy clouds collide
scarlet sun descends
fireflies flitter.

She chants
memories dance
warm rays caress
sea breeze settles
wet sand beneath toes
cool water
on thirsty skin
coconut oil massage.

She chants
memories dance
frogs croak
waves wash
cock crows
leaves rustle
cicadas sing.

She chants
memories dance
sea salt on tongue
brackish guava
juicy Julie mango
coconut water
first mouthful.

She chants
memories dance
ripe breadfruit roasting
charcoal smoke
fresh tangerine
green zest
nostril tingling.

Priestess of the carved head
robe of flamboyant tree,
now might we forget forever
the casual chill of the averted gaze
the whiplash of unbelonging
while memories wash.

Ebony head
dangling earrings
shielding us
from the cold reality
of economic exile.
She chants
memories dance.

Echoes

Voiceless?
                  Less?
The spirits mocked.
You
cannot
afford
to
          be
                  voiceless.
Voice
                            more cr less
voice
                  more voice
amplified
through
terminal stumps
of seventy five million
mutilated tongues
forever
          ever
amplified
including yours
                        yours
                              yours
                                    yours.

Little Sister

Take time, little sister. Yesterday is barely past
and a cradle still rocks
in bright corners of your eyes.
A toy's cranky lullaby still plays.

In the crook of your arm
yellow fleece yearns to snuggle
its teasing odour, your own.

Today, lips used to tasting thumb
wear bloodred lipstick
like a fresh gash.

Swollen flesh bleeds
a scarlet graffiti slash shocking
against such innocent ebony beauty
such still, sad mirrors for eyes. *Little sister, take time.*

Old Woman With Flowers

Inside Brixton station
at evening rush, she stands,
her coat threadbare
string-belted against winter,
an old woman, offering flowers
with dark, unsteady hands.

Her eyes are urns
bearing ashes of hope.
Tossed on a sea of cold faces,
London's commuter tide, they turn
to a full mind's picture,
another time, warmer places.

She sings unheard,
hearing the endless scream
echoing shrill
through time across wide waters:
In yellowing light she weeps still
for lost sons and daughters.

At night when chained hands
pattern the dark
between wake and sleep
only puckered eyelids flutter.
She awaits the final leap.

She tugs at threadbare covers
sighs memory-deep and long
opens wide a moment clear, clear eyes
praying some other takes up her song.

Inner City Tension

So like former times he stands
Another prize black male; another auction block.
Today's setting, London High street, dusk.
Out of multiple images
of careless consumerism
giant logos, chain store names illuminate
a young black male, silhouette
store front framed

Plate glass shattered at his feet,
hands upraised to face the crowd.
Mind track connects history
recorded in technicolour.
'We are come home to roost in your cities.
We know that blood lust
may surface at will
in isolated attacks.

You were there; we are here.
In this reversal no arms trading
no mass violation of persons for labour
no misinterpreting humanity
as naivete. But recognise me.
I am the price of your traffic
in the fittest men, women, children.
Do with me what you will'.

Seared soul, not skin, branded
in a life of denial amongst plenty,
warped too by constant commercials.

Against the pulsating beacon blitz,
the emergency vehicles anti-riot packed,
angry words, glinting eyes
meet force beyond understanding.
Body tension echoes meanings;
and manacles of our times - handcuffs - await.

Rage

No poems left. All caught
in the grey place. Trapped
where the door slammed shut
in your face
stays locked
because you remain black -
not black and exotic;
nor even black and beautiful -

There are no poems left for those
who, black and demanding
therefore, subversive,
resist still, not accepting
the living death on offer.
Only survival remains;
its question mark permanently
cobwebbing overhead.

No poems left. Instead, screaming rage
which I am told does not become poetry.
None will rise triumphant out of the sealed space.
No black muse will intervene knowing full well
that though the body thieves have gone,
spirit thievery thrives! With it,
resistance; death too. This last, alas,
familiar enough; yet a constant surprise.

But, listen good to the silence about you. Note its siren
whistling, its strange cadences
and haunting patterning
its sudden breaking on the consciousness.
Listen good
for rage has its own blend of sound
not always distinguishable
from poetry.

They Say I Had A Son

I wake to silence
a panel of buttons fingertips away
a row of empty beds sighted
like white islands in the distance
for an instant it tames an ocean of fear
after the anxious passage.
And he who has passed?

I listen to silence
thick like midnight humidity
repress the bladder's sensation
press the buzzer. No sound.
I call, a cry both weak and hollow
a sound dripping fear.
I follow with feeble gaze
the life line that is the drip
extended to what looks like a freezer bag.
And the one who has passed?

I wonder how much life
can be contained in a bag,
recognise this is not my death, not yet.
The unplastered hand
peels the skin of covers off
unsteadily fumbles to adjust clothes
unsteadily I raise myself. On chance meeting
will I be told that he has passed on?

Shaky knees mock the silence.
I will myself to clearer brain signals
to steady the too clumsy body
to reach, hold and carry
the life saving contents
a first aim that must succeed, must succeed.

I will this still drugged, heavy body
to human contact;
prepare to pad the long corridor
to hear what must be said. They say I had a son.
Blessed by far are those who get to choose
between life and death.

Some Crumbs Massa
(Unemployment Song One)

I'll work just as hard as I am able
to pick up the crumbs that fall from your table
If you'll   gimme the job

Who me? Uppity! Couldn't be
must be   somebody else you've seen before
Looks just like me   I'm sure

Sm-Art? Which part of me? Ne-ver!
the BA, MSc, Ph.D is only paper
never had any   in the family before   B-OSSS

So I started collectin to make me mother proud
we know it don't make a difference   not in our case...
now   how about the job? Was I suitable?

job not gone already, I know
It say all over the form   EQUAL OPPORTUNITY
but how Equal opps work so? We still always missing the job

I'll work just as hard as I am able PROMISE
to pick up the crumbs that fall from your table if you'll
gimme the job   I'm talking mortage repossession hungry belly

Feedback? Sure   thanks   I didn't sufficiently
draw out during my fifteen minute presentation
that I was actually able to handle   a broom

NO   not body language   PLEASE
cynical remarks during the corporation lunch?
You mean chip on shoulder, style. So, FINALLY black to
basics

But boss, the letter of application states
I've been sweeping floors and streets
half my working life   Could you not assume
I could hold a bloody broom?

Stuff it.   Rubbish job no job low wage job   no security job
all we get anyway pity   equality already hit the ratio10:1
ten jobs for you one for we   black pride not for sale today.
Thanks.

Unemployment Song Two

Ten to one   still murder
I'm not blaming the unemployed
so don't get more depressed
guess   adult life just one   long retirement plan
take it early   take it easy   like the rest of we. Yes.

The protestant work ethic was just another lie fret or cry
still won't get you that elusive evasive share of pie
take another course
NCVQ, MA Computer Technology
How To Appreciate When The Goal Post
Has Been Finally reMoved,   OPEN ACCESS
But do it for you.

Ten to one   still murder but wouldn't you agree
wage slave is only a higher higher form of slavery
Return to basics   cardboard box good enough for you
guess it'll have to do for me   too

Memo

To: White Employer
From: black employable
Keep, capital K, the money in the family.
It's too cliché all that political correctness stuff.
Nobody who matters will notice:
the only black people on your staff are wiping tables
in the canteen apart from the clerical grade ones.
I repeat Keep, capital K, the money within the family.

Consolation

The reason I didn't get the job, mum
remember apprenticeship
some hundred and fifty years ago or so,
when slavery end and we were
apprentice free women and men,
well, this is the age
when blacks are apprentice graduates
apprentice employables
makes a kind of sense don't it?

At least they pay us these days, mum,
when they employ us .
They did never want pay us for we work dem days
did they, mum? Which days? You mean when they didn't
recognise
overseas certificates? You ask who they think they foolin?
Mum, be fair at least they acknowledge,
don't they - they say it time and again-
black people have come such a very very long way.

A Kind of Haunting

You came just exactly as they -
mother, grandmother- said you would
and I charmed, as they warned
let you in, noting only
how fast a pulse could race
how a body glowed as you raised musk.
Little has changed over the years except
this brown woman
standing on the threshold of her knowing.

Two o'clock in the afternoon.
I turn again your photograph
towards me wanting to break the spell.
It doesn't. I am a roaring cane furnace
waiting to consume you.
Afterwards, as the quenching
of a candle flame
I want you extinguished.

Afterwards, I say, go away, please
don't even leave
a dying smoke trail on the wind
for I have poems to write yet
and I can't
with this kind of haunting.

Baby Mother

His baby mother waits no longer for him
She has her council flat, a job
her car, when it works; her plans.

He returns, sour, to number 6A, ground floor
the housing association offered.
'I free, man!' His music shakes
the flat beneath, those on top
and houses on each side.

Proud father of a son, he keeps
a pair of boxing gloves on wardrobe floor
for a gift 'when the boy grow'.

She's past her buggy days now
so busy some times the Venetian blinds
are still drawn and she finds it's night again.
The baby's crying grates tonight. Her head aches.
She has little space for high chairs in her life
But still, school days beckon.

His baby mother had not wanted things this way
the single parenting, these pressures, the needing
the baby always depending. She'd had dreams.

Now, the cold wind blows less fiercely
though if it should again, she knows
she cannot count on anyone else
for her baby; for her.
She bides her time, pregnant this time
not with dreams, but plans. She bides her time.

Survivor

So easy to open my lips, accept the sacrament,
mark the palm print of his touch;

to run my tongue around his words:
each phrase, each pause.

I should have asked instead to journey
to the dark place where his soul

at its most tormented hides, to find there
what might make him so dangerous to me.

Suppose I had noted those poisoned berries
would I have tasted so lovingly?

Dragonfly shadows hovering, mocking me
you carry stolen kisses astride your wings.

Steal away, do for I am a painter of rainbows:
sun and rain together. In my line, we women survive.

Interlude

In between the lusty cry for life
more or less
and the loved one's cry of loss
'Oh Maree, Maree', an interlude,
a fragment of song on the wind,
and such zest for living.

'Three little birds', school children sang
while Marley's song played
and we mere puppets after all
at the Maker's whim.
Spin on, generous Creator
your silken invisible snare.

Knowing our fragility, we weep,
illusions of permanence shattered,
for a young woman passed on,
for trials endured and family too far away.
Only the sliver of song remains
and pincered memories.

An ordinary school girl, Maree
leading across a bridge of hope
land mined, though she could not know.
In public, a quiet smile. At home,
a sister, oh Maree! One who shares.
A daughter, once classmate; colleague.

Today her mother's eyes speak
despite her will, the inevitable pain
the unspoken pride. Immigrant woman,
black woman, West Indian mama.
She had a daughter of such promise
who died in her prime in England.

And we, like children again remember.
In the mercy of time we ask:
how long the page of life?
How short your song, Maree, how bittersweet.
So the cry began by us - since we must -
is echoed by others as we return to dust.

These Streets You Will Know

Ever heard the word 'nigger'
slicing the night's silence
on which dreams ride?
Shattered sleep; hurrying footsteps
running, chasing
male voices calling, 'kill him!"

But, give or take some years,
this is 1993.
What time warped mind
produces such a scene?
I must have dreamt the sobbing;
heard only my own distress.

A cold voice states, ' Leave him.'
We hear grating hatred and
somewhere a male manchild, heart thumping,
breaks the hunters' trail.
But it wasn't so for you, Stephen.
It wasn't so for you.

And even when they found you dying
you were a child invisible
your wounds invisible
your bleeding invisible
only the black male presence visible
spelling danger, even in your dying.

Meanwhile my own son turns sixteen.
This street cloaked in night
threatens to belong to him soon
and with it all the fears
of our repeating history.
My son; our sons.

That night, roused, I checked mentally
my young manchild was in bed. He was.
But it wasn't so for you Doreen.
It wasn't so for you.
And so history moves; an underground river
deep in sore hearts. My son; our sons.

First Earrings

At ten, her ears were pierced
in a large department store,
shiny counters reassuring her mother
on matters of hygiene.

The assistant's thin hand
pointed the gun
at the tiny spot
a mere dot in black biro.

She fired the studs of stars
wearing, a frozen moment,
a sort of a ghostly smile
and her pale hands shook.

Those plastic gloved hands
were not grandmother's hands
with needle, cork
and strong thread

For first earrings
binding girls to mothers
in that infinite maternal chain
crisscrossing half the world.

Each time she'd returned
to the ancestral home
voices asked,
'Ears not pierced yet?'

Now one more daughter belongs.
She looks deep into the mirror
and she smiles
stars.

Madonna

Nurse me
nurse the children
nurse the world.
I am madonna
of the screaming nipples
of the narrative of dirty nappies.
Stay away from me.
I reek of maternal resentment.

Bouquet Of Stems

See I have brought you roses
red for love assumed
though seldom evident.
Watch carefully:
they are tissue wrapped in black.
Look how deft fingers
have snipped the flowers
for scattering!
The bouquet of stems
I leave with thorns intact
in memory
of a shallow marriage
of doomed souls
and scatter the buds
to mark our loss
before I leave.

Warning This Poem Uses Offcuts

These words are taken from the off-cuts
discarded from unsuccessful craftings:
black, racism, prejudice.

How they persist in inscribing themselves!
I have collected sacks full of such off-cuts
spilling out of each: racism, prejudice, black.

I am told that to be taken seriously,
I should avoid such words. Cut them out:
Prejudice, racism, black

Are not indicative of universal experience.
Otherwise, I'd be tempted to keep them in, convinced
there must be some reason for their re-appearing

But publishers insist there is no market in the shires
for such words. In Brixton, London, yes. Liverpool 8, even,
but what of those other places the mainstream reaches?

The liberal minded say they've heard all that before;
it plays on guilt. Too emotive, that's the term. Or, too
cliché
heard in the sixties; the trans Atlantic seventies.

This poem uses oft cut words not suitable for publishing.
I am discarding them once and for all, after today -

There will be no place for such old fashioned
oft cut words, I am sure, in the twenty first century.
I am whittling away at black, prejudice, racism

Found liberally amongst the remnants, the honing.
I am practising instead on daffodils, snow, and
other seasoned universals, not : black, racism, prejudice.

I am learning that poems with black, prejudice, racism
write their own rejection slips
however much you change the ordering.

I am using them today, finally, simply because it seems to me
that black, prejudice, racism, recycled,
could at least be useful as a disposable poem.

Subscribers to the First Edition

Mary Boley
Jacqui Bygrave
Kathy Callanan
Helen Dennison
Mary Elliott
Viv Golding
Heleen Isaacs
Amoafi Kwapong
Marcia Lattery
B.A. Martin
Jenny Mitchell
Thelma Perkins
Lennox Powell
Francis Reneau
Stella V. Ryan
Bybreen Samuels
Annmarie Shadie
Deborah Vaughan
Paulette Williams

My special thanks to Jacob Ross and Amryl Johnson who have been so generous in their encouragement of this publication

Acknowledgements
The following poems have been published previously as indicated: 'Immigrant Woman' in *First Verse* (1992); 'Thoughts of a Cricket Orphan', *New Impact* (Issue 4, 1994); 'Choice' and 'Creation Story' in *Scratch* 12 (1994/95); 'Talkee Mary's Lucid Moments', 'Summer Mango', 'Grandmother', and 'Warning This Poem Uses Offcuts' in *Mango an' Spice* edited by Joan Anim-Addo (Mango Publishing, 1995); 'First Earrings' in *Burning Words, Flaming Images* edited by Kadija Sesay (Saks Media, 1996); 'A Room of My Own' in *The Charleston Magazine* (Spring/Summer, 1996)